A Space Adventure

Written by Brent Morrison

Illustrated by Dominique Albrecht

Flying through the nighttime sky,
Maria saw 10 stars go by.

9 rocky asteroids
were dangerous and busy.

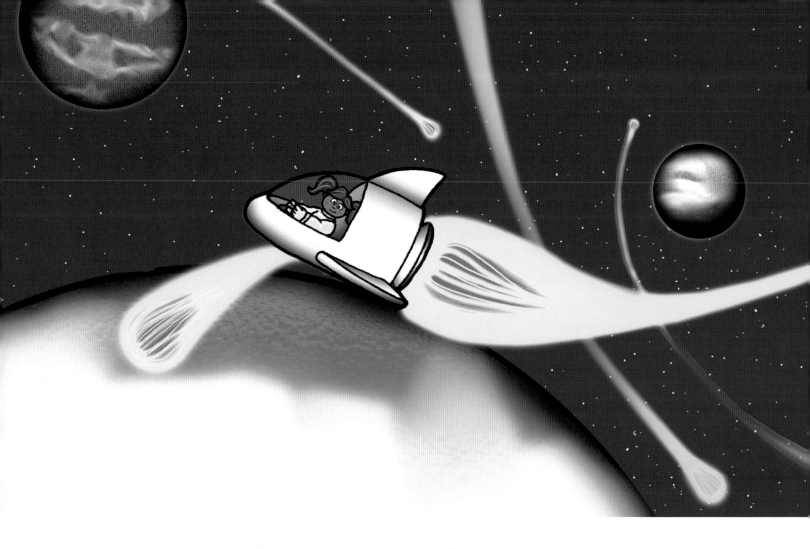

8 spinning planets
made her feel dizzy.

7 bright comets
were chasing their tails.

6 moving satellites
followed their trails.

5 friendly space creatures
waved at her . . .

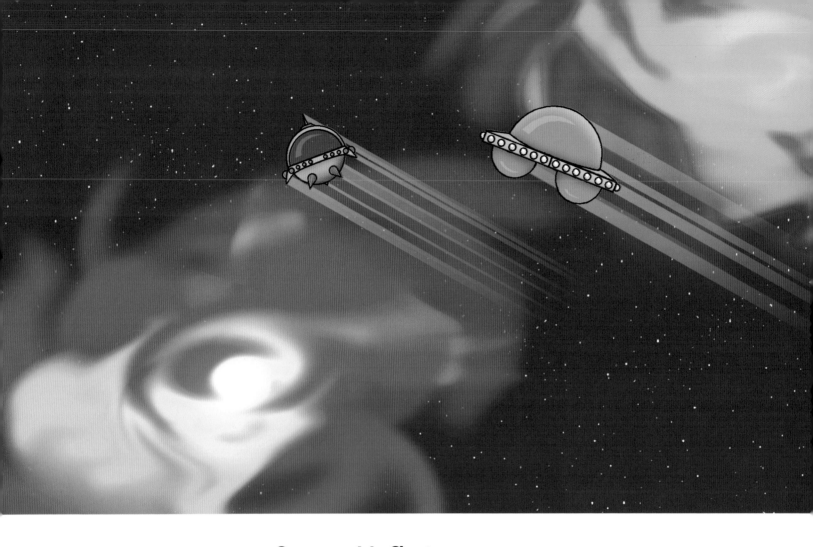

. . . from 4 flying saucers
(if that's what they were).

3 dusty nebulas
used to be suns.

2 swirling galaxies
glittered and spun.

1 planet, Earth,
what a place, what a sight!

"Mom won't believe
all the things I saw tonight."

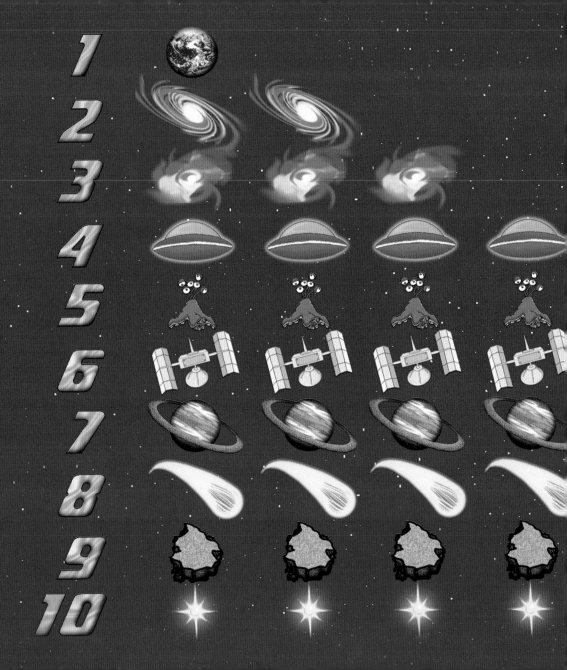